THE 5 MAJOR HABITS OF GREAT PEOPLE

THE ULTIMATE GUIDE TO EFFECTIVELY DEVELOP YOUR POTENTIAL

THE 5 MAJOR HABITS OF GREAT PEOPLE

Albert S. Dolan

COPYRIGHT

THE 5 MAJOR HABITS OF GREAT PEOPLE

Table of content

INTRODUCTION

To succeed, we should develop propensities lined up with great standards.

Indeed, it is like exploring life. While specific little activities can be helpful, getting a handle on a couple of fixed and core values and making a propensity for following them is undeniably more significant.

This is easy to talk about, but not so easy to do. To foster an internal person given good standards, then, at that point, you want to impact how you reliably see and move toward your general surroundings. So, making changes in light of the person's worldview expects that you develop positive routines.

Chapter 1: Start each errand with an ideal result.

We should start with a somewhat sullen mental activity: Imagine that it's three years later, and enough, you've died, unfortunately. Indeed, it's a misfortune. Be that as it may, presently, every one of your companions, family, and partners has accumulated for your memorial service. Every individual alternates venturing to the platform and conveying a tribute. What do you believe they should say regarding you?

Of course, this is hard to contemplate, but at the same time, it's informative. Abruptly, the insignificant subtleties of day-to-day existence liquefy away, and all your genuine needs come into the center. Presently you're pondering your connections, your achievements, and what would you need to abandon.

As this solemn examination shows, taking into account your definitive result is a fundamental part of putting together your life. That is the reason profoundly successful individuals make a propensity for thoroughly considering things - which carries us to our subsequent propensity: start each undertaking with an ideal result.

Whenever you play out an activity, whether large or little, you're doing it two times. Before you genuinely do a cycle, you should initially envision it by conjuring up an arrangement. These plans can be fast and easygoing, similar to a psychological daily agenda of your errands, or thick and point by point, similar to a very much organized strategy.

One way or the other, it means quite a bit to consider the future, as it assists you with exploring the present. Ponder building your fantasy house. Before outlining the house or setting up the rooftop, drafting a blueprint is insightful. All things considered, without a reasonable image of what you're fabricating, the development interaction will be a turbulent fiasco. You'll commit exorbitant errors, squander significant materials, and logically be discontent with the outcome.

It's genuinely simple to apply this guideline to momentary activities. For example, in the expert circle, it's dependably savvy to sort through your week-by-week plan quite a bit early and have clear objectives that you might want to accomplish toward each quarter's end.

Be that as it may, the genuine advantages of this propensity come while making arrangements for the long haul. To do this, envision your ideal life by creating an individual statement of purpose. Do some serious contemplation and work out what you genuinely desire to accomplish, what values you need to maintain, and what you see as a genuine achievement. Utilize this record to quantify your headway and as a manual to assist you with simply deciding. At the point when you know your ideal objective obviously, remaining on the correct path is a lot simpler.

Chapter 2: Put priorities straight.

On Monday morning, and you're at the workplace. Your phone is ringing, the printer's stuck, and you have a report to compose, and an undertaking you intend to draft. What's more, pause - your manager is thumping at your entryway, needing to address you.

What do you handle first?

In any event, when you understand what your objectives are, it's difficult to tell which moves toward take when. Here to help is the second propensity: Put priorities straight. Or on the other hand put in an unexpected way: which is to focus on assignments as per their desperation and significance.

We should discuss how. There are many ways to deal with using time effectively. Some blessing making records; others say you ought to plan your assignments ahead of time. In any case, the genuine mystery to working is sorting out your endeavors by need - and for this, you can utilize a time usage framework.

A time usage lattice is a framework where you list every one of your undertakings as per two aspects: criticalness and significance. To make one, get a piece of paper, and draw an in-pairs network with four boxes. The first box is Quadrant I: undertakings that are dire and significant, similar to an emergency that can't be overlooked. The second box is Quadrant II: assignments that are significant but not critical - think long haul projects like structure client connections. The third box is Quadrant III: this is for assignments that are critical yet not that pivotal, such as picking up the telephone. At last box t is

Quadrant IV: this is for all that is neither critical nor significant, such as playing solitaire.

Whenever you've split every one of your obligations along these lines, it's simpler to see where to concentrate your endeavors. While the things in Quadrant I are significant, actually the positions in Quadrant II merit extraordinary consideration. These are frequently the most ignored because they don't feel as squeezing. Be that as it may, they're as yet significant, and frequently accompany the greatest effectiveness adjustments. Assuming you address them right off the bat, you'll assist with keeping new things from showing up in Quadrant I.

Nobody can do everything alone. Once in a while putting priorities straight expects you to designate things that needn't bother with your touch. Simply be certain not to obsessively hover over. Try not to allow errands; all things being equal, request explicit outcomes. All things considered, with regards to proficiency, the result makes the biggest difference.

Chapter 3: Continuously search for a mutually beneficial situation.

In most football matches there must be one victor and one failure. One group brings back home the prize; the other returns home with basically nothing, regardless of how well they played.

Fortunately, not all everyday issues are this way - where one group should win and the rest come up short. If you utilize cooperative reasoning, most circumstances can be useful together. That is the reason compelling individuals utilize the fourth propensity: guarantee everybody has a positive result.

For life, we structure our connections utilizing specific standards that shape how we collaborate. For some individuals, the prevailing worldview is a success loss perspective. This implies they see each trade, whether individual, business, or other, as a rivalry in which getting what you need, implies different gatherings can't get what they need.

While this worldview is helpful in certain unique circumstances, it's sad in others. It makes everything a contest, transforming likely accomplices into foes. This breeds doubt and disharmony - and, ultimately, makes the two players failures. For instance, envision an outreach group in which just the top-performing individual gets a reward. The rest don't get anything. This is a successful loss game plan that boosts every player to think often just about himself. Individuals who feel like this might conceal leads, or more awful, harm one another. The outcome? Less generally deals.

There is an option in contrast to this, and it's the mutually advantageous worldview. This perspective trenches contest for a coordinated effort. It looks for results that benefit all interested parties. For that outreach group, this could mean giving out rewards just when everybody arrives at individual deals objectives. Like that, one salesman's success is likewise a success for every other person. This mutually beneficial game plan supports correspondence and cooperation and will bring about additional deals and more joyful specialists generally.

What's the most ideal way to guarantee you're continuously searching for the shared benefit? Embrace an overflow attitude. This attitude doesn't seem beneficial things like achievement, bliss, satisfaction, or even benefits as intriguing products. All things being equal, it knows there's in every case a lot for everybody. At the point when you understand there's in every case more worth to be had, it's simpler to search for ways of teaming up on accomplishing it.

With a mutually beneficial mindset, your greatest triumphs come when you see that you're all playing in the same boat.

Chapter 4: Construct more grounded connections by really figuring out others.

Words are foggy, you're continuously squinting, and you can't select a companion from ten stages away. Now is the ideal time to visit the optometrist. Presently, you know how these excursions normally go. You read letters off a graph as the specialist evaluates various focal points. Ultimately, you track down the specific focal point for you.

Be that as it may, imagine a scenario where the specialist adopted an alternate strategy. Imagine a scenario in which, rather than testing your eyes, she gave you her glasses, said, "These worked for me," and left it at that. All things considered, your vision would in any case be foggy, and you'd presumably track down another optometrist.

It sounds ludicrous, yet with regards to correspondence, many individuals carry on that way as a specialist. They offer arrangements before really figuring out the issue. Profoundly successful individuals adopt an alternate strategy, with a fifth propensity: they tune in before they talk.

Great correspondence is at the core of any significant relationship. Sadly, a great many people just improve their talking abilities - that is, they look to be perceived. In any case, that is simply a portion of the image. To truly develop special interactions, you should likewise comprehend. Also, to comprehend somebody, you should figure out how to tune in.

Listening implies more than essentially hearing. It implies getting a handle on someone else's considerations and sentiments on a significant level. The most effective way to do this is by rehearsing compassionate tuning in. This type of listening expects you to tune into somebody's edge of reference both mentally and inwardly. It implies hearing that individual's words, yet additionally uncovering the more profound opinions behind them.

One method for doing this is to hold off on offering guidance until you grasp what somebody is attempting to impart. So rather than answering a tale with your very own account, have a go at recognizing the belief the other individual is attempting to verbalize. This is designated "reflecting," and can be essentially as straightforward as saying, That sounds disappointing, or You feel this is significant. This keeps the discussion focused on the individual you need to comprehend.

In any case, this isn't an easy route or stunt. For compassionate paying attention to work, you should have a true interest in others. It requires investment, exertion, and practice to accurately do. In any case, assuming that you attempt it, individuals will see and value your consideration. They'll frequently respond with sympathy and regard of their own. Over the long run, your connections will turn out to be more open, fulfilling, and significant.

Chapter 5: Make an opportunity to deal with yourself.

Envision yourself as an innovative logger. Consistently, you head into the timberland to begin felling trees. The initial not many are simple. Whack, whack, whack, and down it comes. Notwithstanding, after some time, you notice an upsetting example. Each tree is bringing more slashes to cut down. Before the week's over, bringing down a solitary trunk takes throughout the evening.

What's turned out badly? It's a basic error. While you've been working diligently, you've neglected to deal with your devices. Your dependable hatchet, when smooth and sharp, is currently dull and futile.

As this illustration shows, even the most determined and committed specialists will ultimately wear out on the off chance that they don't enjoy reprieves. Hence, the seventh and last propensity for profoundly powerful individuals is about rest and re-establishment. Make an opportunity to deal with yourself.

As you endeavor to accomplish your desires, it's not difficult to get so up to speed in an outward activity that you disregard to support your prosperity. This is a perilous oversight because without a very much kept up with body, psyche, and soul, all your other powerful propensities will begin to endure. So allotting investment to restoring yourself consistently in four distinct dimensions is urgent.

The first is the actual aspect. This implies dealing with your body with normal activity, legitimate nourishment, and a lot of peaceful rest. Fostering these sound propensities will give you the perseverance to continue to work over the long haul.

The subsequent aspect is profound. Reestablishing this aspect is tied in with reaching out to yourself, your qualities, and the magnificence in your general surroundings. Every day, take a couple of seconds for calm consideration, supplication, or careful reflection. You'll find such practices keep you focused and prepared to deal with misfortune.

The third aspect is mental. Very much like your body, your mind needs ordinary exercises. Remain sharp by continuously discovering new information. Practice new abilities, read new books, or have a go at getting an unknown dialect. These side interests enhance your life and keep you drawn in with your general surroundings.

The fourth and last aspect includes the social and profound parts of your life. Seeking after effectiveness doesn't mean you need to forfeit your public activity. The polar opposite of feeding both your own and proficient relationships is urgent. Check-inCheck-in routinely with friends and family, talk with associates, and play with your youngsters.

On the off chance that you genuinely promise to recharge every one of these aspects, you'll constantly receive the benefits. With this propensity solidly set up, you'll constantly be prepared to go about as a powerful individual.

www.ingramcontent.com/pod-product-compliance
Lightning Source LLC
La Vergne TN
LVHW020544160826
845677LV00015B/4189

9798846767508